The Meaning of Masonry
by Albert Pike

Albert Pike's The Meaning of Masonry
Albert Pike

A Cornerstone Book
Published by Cornerstone Book Publishers
An imprint of Michael Poll Publishing

Cornerstone Book Publishers
New Orleans, LA
www.cornerstonepublishers.com

First Cornerstone Edition - 2003
Second Cornerstone Edition 2014

ISBN: 1613422261
ISBN-13: 978-1-61342-226-7

MADE IN THE USA

The Meaning of Masonry

The Meaning of Masonry

A Lecture
Read at the Request of the Grand Lodge of Louisiana
by Bro. Albert Pike

*The Evil Consequences of Schisms and Disputes
for Power in Masonry,
and of Jealousies and Dissensions
Between Masonic Rites*

1858

SUCH, my brethren, is the subject on which I have been requested to address you. Some who have the interests of Masonry at heart, have thought it was possible to say something upon this subject that might tend to remove erroneous impressions, to increase union and harmony among Masons, and to persuade society at large that its well-being and progress are, to some extent, involved in the advancement and prosperity of Masonry. They have demanded that I should say something; and, though unaffectedly reluctant to do it, my obligation as a Mason bars against me all the avenues of escape, and compels disinclination to yield to the imperative mandate of duty.

It would need no argument to show that to the Masonic Order itself, as to any other order or association, however unpretending and unimportant, intestine dissensions, struggles for the possession of power, jealousies and heart-burnings must necessarily be harmful, retard its growth and progress, repel those who, if it were at peace within itself, would seek to approach its doors; and at first diminish and ultimately destroy its capacity for usefulness. If this were all that I desired to establish, I might say so much and at once conclude.

But we, my brethren, do not believe that this is all. We think that the highest interests of Society, and of the community in which we live, and, perhaps, even interests wider and more general still, those of the Nation, and of humanity at large, are affected and injured, in that which affects and does harm to Masonry. We think that the world without our Temples is deeply interested in the continuance or restoration of peace and harmony within; and that every Mason who encourages or by apathy permits dissensions within the walls that veil our mysteries from the world's eyes, is an enemy, not of Masonry only, but of that world's advancement and prosperity.

It is indeed true that the world at large, the statesmen and the men of business, are not in the habit of attaching much importance to the peaceful operations, the active efforts and silent influences of Masonry. Some even think evil of the order; to others its pretensions are the subject of mirth and food for ridicule; while probably the general impression is that it is a harmless and inoffensive association, rather laudable for its benevolent propensities, its charities, and the assistance its members mutually lend each other; but one in which the world at large is in no wise interested, one whose ceremonies are frivolous, its secrets mere pretence, its titles and dignities absurd, and its dissensions mere childish disputes for barren honours and an empty presidency, fit only to excite the pitying smiles of the grave and the sarcastic laughter of the ill-natured.

Nor is it to be denied, that there is some warrant for this, in the unfortunate proclivity of over-zealous and injudicious brethren to make the history of Masonry remount to the time when Adam, in the Garden of Eden, was Grand Master; to invent fables and manufacture traditions; to invest with a mysterious sanctity the trite commonplaces that all the world is at liberty to know; to give interpretations of symbols that every scholar knows to be untrue and every man of sense knows to be vapid and trivial; in the vain parade of sounding titles and glittering decorations; and more than all, in the angry disputes which rend the bosom of the Order, accompanied with bitter words, harsh epithets and loud denunciations, that give the lie to the combatants' claim of brotherhood, in regard to questions that to the world seem trifling and unreal.

Is society really interested in the peace and progress of Masonry? Has the world a moral right to demand that harmony shall govern in our Temples? Is that a matter which at all concerns the community ? How grave and important are the interests that by our mad dissensions we recklessly put at hazard ? And by what means are peace and harmony to be restored and maintained ?

Such are the questions which it is demanded of me to consider. To do so, it is evidently necessary first to settle what Masonry is, and what its objects are, and by what means and appliances it pro poses to effect those objects.

The well-being of every nation, like that of every individual, is threefold--physical, moral and intellectual. Neither physically, morally, or intellectually is a people ever stationary. Always it either advances or retrogrades; and, as when one climbs a hill of ice, to advance demands continual effort and exertion, while to slide downward one needs but to halt.

The happiness and prosperity of a people consist in advancing on each of the three lines, physical, moral and intellectual, at once- for the day of its downfall draws nearer, even when its intellect is more developed and the works of its genius are more illustrious, and while its physical comforts increase, if its moral progress does not keep pace with its physical and intellectual; and yet without the last, the two first do not mark the loftiest condition of a great people.

That institution deserves the title of " public benefactor," which by a system of judicious charities and mutual assistance diminishes the sum total of haggard want and destitution, and relieves the public of a portion of the burden which the necessities of the poor and shelterless impose upon it: for it thus aids the physical advancement of the people.

It still more deserves the title, if in addition, it imperatively requires of its members the strict and faithful performance of all those duties towards their fellow-men as individuals, which the loftiest and purest morality enjoins; and so is the potent auxiliary of the laws, and the enforcer of the moral precepts of the great Teacher who preached the Sermon on the Mount: for it thus labours for the moral elevation of the people.

And still more, if its initiates are also, and of necessity, devoted to the true interests of the people if they are the soldiery of Liberty, Equality and Brotherhood, and at the same time of good government, of good order, and of the laws, that made by the representatives of all, for the general good of all, must be implicitly obeyed by all: for thus again it aids in elevating still higher the moral character of the people.

And most of all, if in addition to all this, it strives to elevate the people intellectually, by teaching those who enter its portals the profoundest truths of Philosophy, and the wisdom of the Sages of every age; a rational conception of the Deity; of the universe that He has made, and of the laws that govern it; a true estimate of Man himself, of his freedom to act, of his dignity and his destiny.

I mean to speak only of what Masonry teaches; and to set up no extravagant pretensions in its behalf. That its precepts are not fully obeyed by its initiates, in no wise detracts from their value or excellence; any more than the imperfect performance of its votaries detracts from the excellence of religion. The theory and the intentions of every man that lives are better and purer than his practice-I do not say they are unfortunately so; for it is one of the great kindnesses of Providence, and a most conclusive proof of God's existence and infinite benevolence, that the worst as well as the purest of men has ever which he must perforce always struggle to reach, an ideal and exemplar of a rarer excellence than he can ever attain to, strive and struggle as he may. It has been well and truly said, that even Hypocrisy is the involuntary homage which vice pays to virtue.

The Masons who do not live up to the teachings of their Order, proves only that they are men; that, like other men, they are weak with the frailties of feeble human nature; and that in the never ceasing struggle with their passions and the mighty circumstances that environ us all, it is often their lot to be discomfited. If the doctrines of Masonry are good, they of necessity have their effect, and are never taught in vain. For not in vain are the winged seeds of Truth ever sown; and if committed to the winds, God sees to it that they take root somewhere and grow.

To inquire what Masonry is, is not only to seek to know its history, its antecedents, and its statistics, but more and chiefly to inquire what are its morals and its philosophy. This latter is the inquiry that I have proposed to myself to answer; but as its importance to the world without depends upon the extension of the Order, the number of its members, and its permanency, I must first, and with that view alone, say a few words as to the former. If the Masonic Order were merely a thing of yesterday, ephemeral, and to pass away to-morrow; if it were local, and confined to one country or to men of one faith, or if the number of its initiates were small, and therefore its capacity for good or evil limited, it would be comparatively unimportant to inquire what were its morality and its philosophy.

It is not ephemeral or transitory. I will not claim that it was coeval with Noah or with Enoch, or that its Lodges were held within the holy walls of the first Temple at Jerusalem, or even that it arose during the times of the Crusades. It is enough to say that its origin is hidden in the mists and shadows of antiquity. The Arab builds into his rude walls the carved blocks that once were a part of Babylonian palaces, when Ezekiel prophesied, and when Daniel interpreted the dreams of Kings: the stones hewn by the Old Etruscans before Romulus slew his brother and built the first wall for Rome, may be still seen in the works of Roman architects: and so in our Rituals, attesting the antiquity of the Order, remain embedded words now obsolete, their meaning long forgotten and only recently rediscovered.

We know from historical testimony that the Order existed in England and Scotland in the seventeenth century, and was introduced into France in the year 1721, one hundred and thirty-seven years ago. As early as the year 1787, it had extended into almost every State in Europe, into the East and West Indies and Turkey; and it was estimated that there were then 3,217 Lodges, numbering at least 200,000 members. Then the United States were in their first childhood, chiefly confined to a narrow strip of country along the Atlantic coast, and there and in Canada there were estimated to be but 85 Lodges.

Now, in our thirty-one States, the District of Columbia, and our Territories there are thirty-six Grand Lodges- and in the whole nation not far from 4,200 Lodges, besides other Subordinate Bodies of all the Rites; with a membership of not less than

5

140,000 persons. In every Christian country on the globe our Temples are frequented; and in Turkey, India and Persia, the Mohammedan bows before the altar of Masonry. In England, France, Scotland, Ireland, Germany and Switzerland, the Order has continued to advance. Though Popes have excommunicated and the Inquisition has persecuted, Masonry yet lives in Spain, and under the shadow of the Papal throne- and when in Naples it has been unsafe to meet on land, Lodges have been held upon the open sea, in sight of the thousand lights of the city and of the pharos of Messina, with the starry heavens alone for the covering of the triangular Lodge of boats, from which up to Heaven rose the sweet incense of Masonic prayer.

The greatest, the wisest and the best of men in every country have adorned the great Order in both ancient and modern times; and united zealously in its labours. Statesmen, soldiers, advocates, scholars, poets, artists, the merchant, the mechanic, and the labourer, have for one hundred and thirty-seven years at least, " met in our Lodges upon the level, and parted on the square." PAUL JONES, LAFAYETTE and WASHINGTON were Masons: FRANKLIN sat with LALANDE in the same Lodge in which HELVETIUS had worn the apron. Almost all the great marshals and generals of Napoleon, including the three kings, Joseph, Murat and Bernadotte knew the mystic numbers, and made the French and Scottish Rites illustrious. Natural Science contributed to Masonry a Lacepede, Painting, a Horace Vernet, Music, a Meyerbeer, the Stage, Talma; the Bar Philippe Dupin, his not less illustrious elder Brother and Odilon Barrot. In other countries Masonry counted its distinguished names, too numerous to mention and at the present day, in our own, its initiates occupy the high places of the country, hold the helm of the ship of State, sit in the Departments of State, War, the Interior, and others, preside on the Bench, and represent our country at foreign courts.

In Europe it has founded public libraries, established free schools, given rewards for eminent acts of virtue and heroism, established homes for Masons poor and destitute, fed the hungry, clothed the naked, and been the friend of the oppressed and unfortunate.

In our own country, it follows in good faith the same

path. It establishes schools and founds academies, and its five thousand two hundred Lodges are so many centres from which charity flows in all directions like the light, and whose exchequers are rich with the gratitude of widows, and the tearful thanks of orphans. And prominent above all, like a great light that sends its rays far across the waters, stands THE LOUISIANA RELIEF LODGE, that noblest of Masonic institutions, opening wide its doors to the sick, the destitute, the friendless stranger, and doing honour to Masonry and to the State.

With this mere glance at the history, the antecedents, the personnel and the statistics of Masonry, I must be content. It is sufficient to show that it is of some importance to this community, to the Union and the world, to know what are the morals and philosophy taught by this great, permanent and widely extended Order.

What then, is the morality of Masonry? Listen, and you shall learn. Masonry says to its initiate: "BE CONTENT. Compare not your condition with the few above you, but with the thousands with whom you would not by any means change your fortune and condition. A soldier must not think himself unprosperous, if he be not successful as Alexander or Wellington; nor any man deem himself unfortunate that he hath not the wealth of Rothschild, but rather let the former rejoice that he is not lessened like the many generals who went down, horse and man, before Napoleon; and the latter, that he is not the beggar, who in the bleak winter wind holds out his tattered hat for charity. There may be many who are richer and more fortunate; it is certain that there are many thousands who are very miserable, compared to you."

But a Mason's contentedness must by no means be a mere contented selfishness; like him, who, comfortable himself, is indifferent to the discomfort of others. There will always be in this world wrongs to forgive, sufferings to alleviate, sorrows asking for sympathy, necessities and destitution to relieve, and ample occasion for the exercise of active charity and beneficence. And he who sits unconcerned amidst it all, perhaps enjoying his own comforts and luxuries the more, by contrasting them with the hungry and ragged misery and shivering wretchedness of his fellows, is not contented, but only unfeeling and brutal.

7

It is the saddest of all sights upon this earth, that of a man, lazy and luxurious, or hard and penurious, to whom want appeals in vain, and suffering cries in an unknown tongue. The man whose hasty anger hurries him into violence or crime, is not half so unworthy to live. This is the faithless steward, that embezzles what is given him in trust for the penniless and impoverished among his brethren. The true Mason must be, and must have a right to be, content with himself; and he can be so, only when he lives, not for himself alone, but for others, who need his assistance and have a claim upon his sympathy.

"Charity," says a fine old writer, "is the great channel through which God passes all his mercies upon mankind. For we receive absolution of our sins in proportion to our forgiving our brother. This is the rule of our hopes, and the measure of our desire in this world; and on the day of death and judgment, the great sentence upon mankind shall be transacted according to our alms, which is the other part of charity. God Himself is LOVE; and every degree of charity that dwells in us, is the participation of the Divine Nature."

These principles Masonry reduces to practice and by them it expects its initiates to be guided and governed. It says to them, in the words of the great Roman: "Men in no respect nearly approach to the Deity, as when they confer benefits on men. To serve and do good to as many as possible--there is nothing greater in your fortune than that you should be able, and nothing finer in your nature than that you should be desirous, to do this." It expects every man to do something, within and according to his means; and if not alone, then by combination and association. A Lodge may aid in founding a school or an academy; and if not, it can at least educate one boy or girl the child of a poor or departed Brother. And it should never be forgotten, that in the poorest unregarded child that seems abandoned to ignorance and vice, may slumber virtue, intellect and genius and that in rescuing from the mire and giving him the means of education and development, the Lodge may confer on the world as great a benefit as was given it by John Faust, the boy of Mentz, who revealed to it the art of Printing.

For we never know the importance of the act we do. The

daughter of Pharaoh little thought what she was doing for the human race, and the vast unimaginable consequences that depended on her charitable act, when she drew the little child of a Hebrew woman from among the rushes that grew along the bank of the Nile, and determined to rear it as her own. How often has an act of charity, costing the doer little, given to the world a great painter, a great sculptor, a great musician, a great inventor? How often has such an act developed the ragged boy into a benefactor of his race! For there is no law, thank God! that limits the returns that shall be reaped from a single good deed. The widow's mite may not only be as acceptable to God, but may produce as large results, as the rich, costly offering.

Masonry inculcates upon the master, care and kindness for the slave whom God has placed in his power and under his protection. It teaches to the employers of other men, in mines, manufactories and workshops, consideration and humanity for those who depend upon their labour for their bread, and to whom want of employment is starvation, and overwork is fever, consumption and death. While it teaches the employed to be honest, punctual and faithful, as well as respectful, and obedient to all proper orders, it also teaches the employers that every man or woman that desires to work, has a right to have work to do- and that these, and those who from sickness or feebleness, old age or infancy, are not able to work, have a right to be fed, clothed, and sheltered from the inclement elements- that he commits an awful sin against Masonry and in the sight of God, if he closes his workshop or factory, or ceases to work his mine, when they do not yield him what he considers sufficient profit, and so dismisses his workmen and workwomen to starve; or when he reduces their wages to so low a standard that they and their families cannot therewith be fed and clad and comfortably housed; or by over-work must give him their blood and life in exchange for the pittance of their wages; and that his duty as a Mason and a Brother peremptorily requires him to continue to employ those who else will be pinched with hunger and cold, or must resort to theft and vice and to pay them fair wages, though it may reduce or annul his profits, or even eat into his capital; for God has but LOANED him his wealth, and made him His almoner and agent to invest it.

Not only in their charities, but in every other manner,

9

Masonry will have its initiates to be GENEROUS; not careful to return no more than they receive, but preferring that the balance upon the ledger of benefits shall be in their favour. He, it holds, who has received payment in full for all the benefits and favours that he has conferred, is like a spendthrift who has consumed his whole estate, and laments over an empty exchequer. He who requites our favours with ingratitude, adds to, instead of diminishing our wealth, and he who cannot return a favour, is equally poor, whether that inability arise from poverty of spirit and sordidness of soul or actual pecuniary need.

If he is wealthy who has large sums invested, and the mass of whose fortune consists in obligations by which other men promise to pay him money, he is still more so, to whom many owe large returns of kindnesses and favours. Beyond a moderate sum each year, the rich man merely interests his means, and that which he never uses is still, like favours unrequited and kindnesses unreciprocated a real portion of his fortune. It is the Mason's part to protect the feeble against the strong, and the defenceless against rapacity and craft; to succour and comfort the poor, and be the guardian, under God, of His innocent and helpless wards- to value friends more than riches or fame, and gratitude more than money or power; and so to be the true nobleman by God's patent, his escutcheon and quarterings to be found in Heaven's great book of Heraldry; to be liberal, but only of that which is his own; to be generous, but only when he has first been just; to give, when it involves the deprivation of a luxury or a comfort.

"I will not acknowledge as an initiate," Masonry declares, " the man who is not disinterested and generous, not only in acts, but in his opinions of men, and his constructions of their conduct. He who is selfish and grasping, or censorious and ungenerous, will not remain within the strict limits of Honesty and Truth, but will shortly commit injustice. He who loves himself too much, must needs love others too little; and he who is inclined to harsh judgment, will not long delay to give unjust judgment, and afterwards or not at all, hear the case. The worldly, the covetous and the sensual; the man governed by inclination and not by duty; the unkind, severe, censorious or injurious in the relations or intercourse of life; the unfaithful parent or undutiful child; the cruel master or faithless servant; the treacherous friend, bad neighbour, or bitter and ungenerous competitor, may wear the white apron

10

of the Mason, and rejoice in all the titles of the Order; but he wanders at a great distance from the true Masonic Light."

Next, Masonry required of its Initiates, FIDELITY. "Truth plighted is ever to be kept." It does not cease to repeat them, was an axiom even among Pagans. The virtuous Roman said: "Either let not that which seems expedient be base, or if it be base, let it not seem expedient." The word of a Mason, like that of a Knight in the times of Chivalry, once given, ought to be sacred; and the judgment of his Brethren, upon him who violates his pledge, should be stern as the judgments of the Roman Censors against him who violated his oath. Calamity should always be chosen rather than baseness; and we should prefer to die rather than be dishonoured. INDUSTRY and HONESTY are virtues peculiarly inculcated in Masonry. When the arrogant Stuarts sat upon the throne of England, and the Bourbons on that of France, each claiming to rule by Divine right; when Republican Government was more remote from actual life than Utopia or the New Atlantis; when Nobility thought it was born to rule, and the people to toil and serve; when Rank and Caste and Privilege looked down with lordly contempt upon the leathern apron of the artisan and the frieze jerkin of the labourer, THE GREAT ORDER wrought silently in its degree of Apprentice, Craftsman and Master Mason or Builder- adopted for itself a democratic system of government; and for the successor of the Demi-gods and Princess of the old legends of the Mysteries, selected an humble artisan, the son of a poor widow of Tyre an industrious and honest man, cunning to work in brass and iron; and represented him as the Peer of Kings. The history of the world hardly offers a more significant and extraordinary lesson.

As the bees have no love for drones, so true Masons have none for the idle and lazy, for those who are so, are already useless, and in the way to become dissipated and vicious; and perfect honesty, which ought to be the common qualification of all, is more rarely met with than diamonds. To do earnestly and steadily, to do faithfully and honestly that which we have to do--perhaps this wants but little, when looked at from every point of view, of including the whole body of the moral law.

We think, at the age of twenty, that life is much too long for that which we have to learn and do; and that there is an al-

11

most fabulous distance between our age and that of our Grand-father. But when, at the age of sixty, if we are fortunate enough to reach it, or unfortunate enough, as the case may be, and according as we have used or wasted our time, we halt and look back along the way that we have come, and cast up and try to balance our accounts with Time, we find that we have made Life much too short, and thrown away a large portion of our days. We then in our mind deduct from the sum total of our years, the hours that we unnecessarily have spent in sleep; the waking hours each day, during which the surface of the mind's pool has not been stirred or ruffled by a single thought; the days that we have got rid of as we could, to attain some real or fancied object that lay beyond, in the way between which and us stood irksomely and intervening days; and the hours misspent and worse than wasted, in folly and dissipation; and we acknowledge with many a sigh, that we could have learned and done, in half a score of years well spent, more than we have learned and done in our forty years of manhood.

To learn and to do I This is the soul's work here below. The soul grows, as truly as an oak grows. As the tree takes the air and the particles that float in the air, the dew and the rain, and the food that in the earth lies piled around its roots; and by its mysterious chemistry transmutes them to sap and fibre, into wood and leaf, and flower and fruit, and taste and colour and perfume; and the soul drinks in knowledge, and by a divine alchemy changes what it learns into its own substance, and develops itself from within outwardly, and grows, with an inherent Force and Power like those which lie hid in the small germ of the acorn.

To sleep little, and to study much; to say little, and to hear and think much; to learn, that we may be able to do; and then to do, earnestly and vigorously, whatever is required by Duty, by the interests of our fellows, our country and mankind,--these are the duties which Masonry prescribes to its initiates.

It requires of them "honesty in contracts sincerity in affirming, simplicity in bargaining, and faithfulness in performing." It says to them, in the terse language of an old writer, " Lie not at all, neither in a little thing nor in a great, neither in the substance nor in the circumstance, neither in word nor deed; that is, pretend not what is false; aver not what is untrue; and let the measure of your affirmation or denial be the understanding of your contractor."

"That any man should be the worse for us, and our direct act, and by our intention, is against the rule of our equity, of justice and of charity." We, then, do not that to others, which we might reasonably wish they should do unto us; for we grow richer upon the ruins of their fortune. The good Mason does not wish to receive any thing from another, without returning him an equivalent: and by that simple principle, Masonry discountenances bets and gaming among its members; while it frowns upon him who takes wages or fees for a work that he is incompetent to do, or demands more than his services are honestly and according to the custom worth; upon the merchant who sells an inferior article for a sound price upon the speculator who makes the needs and distresses of other men his exchequer.

It says to every Mason: " It should be our earnest desire so to live and deal and act, that when it comes to us to die, we shall be able to say, and our consciences to adjudge, that no man on earth is poorer, because we are richer- that what we have, we have honestly earned or purchased; and that no man, and more especially no widow or orphan, can stand up before God, and claim that by the Rules of Equity administered in His great Chancery, this house in which we die, this land that we devise among our heirs, this money which, enriches those who survive to bear our name, is his or hers, and not ours, and we in that Great Forum are only their Trustees. For it is most certain that God is just, and will sternly enforce every such trust; and that to all whom we despoil, to all whom we defraud, to all from whom we take anything whatever without full and fair equivalent, He will decree an adequate and ample compensation."

"Be careful," then, it says to every Brother, "that thou receive no wages, here or elsewhere, that are not thy due. For if thou dost, thou wrongest someone, by taking that which in God's Chancery belongs to him; and whether that which thou takest thus, be wealth or rank, or influence or reputation."

Again, it says to him: "Be zealous and faithful I be disinterested and benevolent I Act the peacemaker, in case of dissentions, disputes and quarrels among the Brethren. DUTY is the

13

moral magnetism that controls and guides the true Mason's course over the tumultuous seas of Life. Whether the Stars of Honour, Reputation and Reward do or do not shine; in the light of day, or in the darkness of the night of trouble and adversity; in calm or storm, that unerring magnet still shows him the true course to steer, and indicates with certainty whereaway lies the port, which not to reach involves shipwreck and dishonour. He follows implicitly its silent bidding, as the mariner, when land is for many days not in sight, and the ocean, without path or land-mark, howls angrily around him, follows the silent bidding of the needle, as though it were God's finger, pointing unerringly to the North. To perform that Duty, whether the performance be re-warded or unrewarded, is his sole care; nor does it matter to him, though of this performance there may be no witnesses, and though what he has done will be forever unknown to all man-kind.

Times change, and circumstances; but Virtue (in the origi-nal meaning of the old Roman word Virtus, manliness) and Duty, ever remain the same The evils to be confronted only take another shape; and are developed in a different form. There is the same need now of Truth and Loyalty, as there was in the days of knight-hood. In no age of the world has man had better opportunity than now to display a lofty manliness and noble heroism

When a fearful epidemic ravages a city, and death is in-haled with the air men breathe; when the living scarcely suffice to bury the dead; most men flee in abject terror, to return and live, respectable and influential, when the danger has passed away. But the old knightly spirit of devotion and disinterested-ness and contempt of death, still lives, and is not extinct in the human heart. Everywhere, a few are found to stand firmly and unflinchingly at their posts, to front and defy the danger, not for money, nor to be honoured for it nor to protect their own house-hold; but from mere humanity, and to obey the unerring dictates of duty. Brethren of some benevolent Order or Association, or philanthropists that belong to no Order, they nurse the sick, breathing the pestilential atmosphere of the Hospital. They ex-plore the dens of want and misery. Gentle as women, they soften the pangs of the dying, and feed the lamp of life in the convales-cent. They perform the sad offices to the dead; and they seek for all no other reward than the approval of their own consciences.

14

Like one, a member of THE GREAT ORDER, whom because he lives among us, and seeks no such acknowledgment, I will not name, they go as volunteers to distant cities, where the cross is marked on every door, the pestilence crouches in every house, and dismay and terror are in every heart; there to attend the sick and relieve the suffering; and when the ghastly destroyer has passed away, a STATE engraves their names upon the eternal tablets of its memory, and mothers teach their children to bless them and remember them in their prayers.

These obey the Masonic law of Duty;--these, and the captain who remains at his post on board his shattered ship, until the last boat, loaded to the water's edge with passengers and crew, has parted from her side; and then, like Herndon, goes calmly down with her into the mysterious depths of the ocean; the pilot who stands at the wheel while the swift flames eddy round him, and scorch away his life; the fireman who climbs the blazing walls, and plunges amid the flames, to save the lives of those who have upon him no claim by tie of blood, of friendship, or even of ordinary acquaintance,-- these, and all men, who, set at the post of duty stand there manfully, to die, if need be, but not to desert their post.

THE GREAT ORDER insists that its Initiates shall be Just; that faithfully using that moral faculty, the conscience, and applying it to existing relations and circumstances, they shall develop it and all its kindred powers, and so deduce the duties that, out of these relations and these circumstances, and by them limited and qualified, arise and become obligatory upon us; and to learn justice, the law of right, the Divine rule of conduct for human life. It says, in part in the words of a profound if erratic thinker: "Every departure from real, practical justice, is no doubt attended with loss to the unjust man, though the loss is not reported to the public. Injustice, public or private, like every other sin and wrong, is inevitably followed by its consequences, which men style its punishment. The selfish, the grasping, the inhuman, the fraudulently ungenerous employer and the cruel master, are detested by the great popular heart; while the kind master, the liberal employer, the generous, the humane and the just, have the good opinion of all men; and even Envy is a tribute to their virtues. Men honour all who stand up for truth and right, and never shrink. The world builds monuments to its patriots, and

15

tears down the statues of its knaves. Four great Statesmen, organizers of the right, embalmed in stone, look down upon the Lawgivers of France, as they pass to their hall of legislation, silent orators to tell how nations love the just. How we love the marble lineaments of those just judges, JAY and MARSHALL, that look so calmly towards the living Bench of the Supreme Court of the United States! What a monument WASHINGTON has built in the heart of America; and all the world, not because he dreamed of an impracticable ideal justice, but by his constant and successful effort to be practically just.. "But necessity only, and the greatest good of the greatest number, can legitimately interfere with the dominion of absolute and ideal justice. Government should not foster the strong, at the expense of the weak, nor protect the capitalist and tax the labourer. The powerful should not seek a monopoly of development and enjoyment; not prudence only, and the expedient for to-day should be appealed to by statesmen, but conscience and the right: justice should not be forgotten in looking at interest; nor political morality neglected for political economy; we should not have national housekeeping, instead of national organization on the basis of right.."

"We may well differ as to the abstract right of many things; for every such question has many sides, and few men look at all of them; many only at one. But we all readily recognize cruelty, unfairness, inhumanity, partiality, over-reaching, hard dealing, by their ugly and familiar lineaments. We do not need to sit as a Court of Errors and Appeals, to revise and reverse God's Providences in order to know and to hate and despise them."

And so it says, and again partly in the words of the same Thinker: "A sentence is written against all that is unjust: written by God in the nature of man, and in the nature of the universe; because it is in the nature of God. Fidelity to your faculties, trust in their convictions--that is justice to yourself a life in obedience thereto, that is justice towards men. No wrong is really successful. The gain of injustice is a loss; its pleasure, suffering. Iniquity often seems to prosper, but its success is its defeat and shame. After a long while, the day of reckoning ever comes, to nation as to individual. The knave deceives himself. The miser, starving his brother's body, starves also his own soul, and at death shall creep out of his great estate of injustice, poor and naked and miserable. Who so escapes a duty, avoids a gain Outward judgment often fails, inward justice never- and we ever see a continual and progressive triumph of the Right."

TRUTH, a Mason is early told, is a Divine attribute, and the foundation of every virtue; and frankness, reliability, sincerity, straightforwardness, plain dealing, are but different modes in which Truth develops itself. Our lectures say, " The dead, the absent, the innocent, and those that trust him, no Mason will deceive willingly. To all these he owes a nobler justice, in that they are the most certain trials of Human Equity. "Only the most abandoned of men," said CICERO, "would deceive him who would have remained uninjured, if he had not trusted. All the noble deeds that have beat their marches through succeeding ages, have proceeded from men of Truth and genuine courage. The man who is always true, is both virtuous and wise, and thus possesses the greatest guards of safety; for the law has not power to strike the virtuous; nor can fortune subvert the wise."

In this age of exaggeration and insincere profession; when books are written and published and even read, whose object is to teach the rising generation how easily a fortune may be made by entrapping gulls with lies; and when for one to give a true account or a fair one of the speech or argument made against his opinions or his party, is a thing so rare, that the recurrence of the phenomenon at long intervals, goes far to make the most confirmed and incurable infidel yield up his unbelief in miracles:--in this age when falsehoods, told for effect, and the faculty of utterance whereof is a gift, that yields a comfortable revenue can get printed by steam and travel on the invisible wings of the lightning,--Masonry still adheres to its old morals, and says to its initiates: " Speak thou always the simple Truth, no more and no less; or else speak not at all." And it adds: " Be thou no talebearer, nor retailer of scandal; for he who is so, is certain often to go beyond the truth."

With the errors and even the sins of other men that do not personally affect us or ours, and need not our condemnation to be odious, we have really nothing to do. The journalist has no patent that makes him the censor of morals. There is no obligation resting on us to trumpet forth our disapproval of every injudicious, improper or wrongful act, that every other man commits. One is not obliged to enlist in the police, or play the spy and the informer.

17

"One ought," a great German says, "to write or speak against no other in this world. Each man in it has enough to do, to watch and keep guard over himself. Each of us is sick enough in this great Lazaretto and journalism and political writing constantly reminds us of a scene once witnessed in a little hospital; where it was horrible to hear how the patients mockingly reproached each other with their disorders and infirmities; how one, who was worn to a skeleton by consumption, jeered at another who was bloated by dropsy; how the leper laughed at his room-mate's cancer of the face; and this one again at his neighbour's paralysis; until at last the delirious fever-patient sprang out of his bed, and tore away the coverings from the wounded bodies of his companions; and nothing was to be seen but hideous misery and mutilation." If we would but look at it aright, is the business of parading before all the world every domestic tragedy and every act of disreputable villainy, any less disgusting, or any more profitable to humanity ?

Very often the censure bestowed upon men's acts, by those who have elected and commissioned themselves keepers of the Public Morals, is undeserved. Often, it is not only undeserved; but praise is due instead of censure; and when deserved, it is always extravagant and therefore unjust..

Even the man who does wrong and commits errors, often has a quiet home, a peaceful fireside, a gentle, loving wife and innocent children, who do not know of his misdeeds, past and long repented of, or present and hereafter to be atoned for by sincere penitence and mighty agonies and bitter remorse; or, if they do, do love him all the better, because being mortal he hath erred, and being in the image of God he hath repented, or will, persuaded by their soft and gentle influences, repent and make atonement, if no uninvited censor thrusts himself between him and them That every blow aimed at this husband and father, strikes brutally at the bosoms of the wife and daughters, and makes them, though innocent, to partake of the shame which falls on him, does not stay the hand of the modern guardian of public morals- but, brave as Caesar, he strikes and slays, and then calls on those to whose vicious appetites he had pandered, to admire and praise him for the generous and manly act..

"If ye seek," says an old writer, "for high and strained car-
riages, you shall for the most part meet with them in low men. Arrogance is a weed that ever grows on a dunghill. There is no arrogance so great as the proclaiming of other men's errors and
faults, by those who understand nothing but the dregs of actions,
and who make it their business to besmear deserving fames." It is
no more honourable now than heretofore, for one to become a
perpetual spy upon the actions of other men, and a general talebearer, even if one is fortunate enough to own a press and types,
and so can retail his scandal to a multitude instead of one. Imagine
only, a gentleman, making it his trade whereby to earn a living, to
fish in all the moral sewers of a city for all the instances of low vice
and disgusting depravity, that for the credit of human nature
ought to be ignored; and then to stand at the street corners and
retail them orally to all the prurient and bestial who would listen,
and for his trouble deposit in his palm a sixpence!

The same old writer adds, and his words are singularly
applicable to-day: "Their malice makes them nimble-eyed, apt to
note a fault and publish consciously believes, is truth, to him; --
these are it and with a strained construction to deprave the mortal
enemies of that Fanaticism which those things that the doer's in-
tents have told his persecutes for opinion's sake, and initiates cru-
sades soul were honest. They set the vices of other men on high,
for the gaze of the world. If they cannot wound upon proofs, they
will do it upon likelihoods; and if not upon them, they manufacture lies, as God created the world, out of nothing; knowing that
the multitude will believe them, because affirmations are apter to
win belief, than negatives to uncredit them; and that a lie travels
faster than an eagle flies, while contradiction lags after it at a
snail's pace, and halting, never overtakes it."

In his words, Masonry lays down its rule: "If there be virtues, and thou art called upon to speak of him that owns them, do
thou tell them forth impartially; and if there be vices mixed with
them, be thou content the world shall know them by some other
tongue than thine. For if the evil doer himself deserve no pity
(which Christ, who died for him, does not say), his wife, his par-
ents, or his children, or other innocent persons who love him may."

19

The Mason is devoted to the cause of LIBERALITY and TOLERATION, against Fanaticism and Persecution, political and religious; to that of EDUCATION, INSTRUCTION and ENLIGHTENMENT against Error, Barbarism and Ignorance.

TOLERATION, holding that every other man has the same right to his opinion and faith, that we have to ours; LIBERALITY, holding that, as no human being can say with certainty, in the clash and conflict of hostile faiths and creeds, what is Truth, or that he is surely in possession thereof; so every one should feel that it is quite possible that another, equally honest and sincere with himself, and yet holding the contrary opinion, may himself be in possession; and that whatever one firmly and consciouly be-lieves, is truth, to him; - these are the mortal enemies of that Fa-naticism which persecutes for opinion's sake, and initiates cru-sades against whatever it deems, in its imaginary holiness to be contrary to the law of God.

And EDUCATION, INSTRUCTION and ENLIGHTEN-MENT are the only certain means by which Intolerance and Fa-naticism can be rendered powerless.

No true Mason scoffs at honest convictions, and an ardent zeal in the cause of Truth and justice. But he absolutely denies the right of any man to assume the prerogative of Deity, and con-demn his Brother's faith and opinions as heretical and deserving to be punished. Nor does he approve the course of those who en-danger the peace of great nations, and the solid interests of his own race, by indulging in the cheap luxury of a chimerical and visionary philanthropy; who draw their robes around them to avoid contact with their fellows, and think themselves nearer to heaven by proclaiming their own holiness.

For he knows that Intolerance and Bigotry have been infi-nitely greater curses to mankind than Ignorance and Error. He does not forget that Galileo was denied the free enjoyment of light and air, because he averred that the earth moved; and that, two centuries ago, the rack and the stake would have been the reward of Agassiz and Lyell. Better any error than persecution I Better any belief or opinion, however irrational and absurd, than the thumbscrew and the *auto da fe*! And he knows also how unspeakably absurd it is for a creature, to whom himself, and everything within and around him are mysteries to torture and even slay others, because they do not think as he does in regard to the profoundest of all those mysteries, the least of which it is utterly beyond the comprehension of either to understand.

It holds, in the language of a wise writer, "that virtue by no means consists in the thinking or believing, which is an accidental, inevitable matter, where the man is sincere; but in the doing, which depends solely on himself. Virtue is but heroic bravery to do the thing thought to be true, in spite of all enemies of flesh or spirit, or temptations or menaces. Man is accountable for the uprightness of his doctrine, but not for the rightness of it. Devout enthusiasm is far easier than a good action. The end of Thought is action, and the sole purpose of Religion is an ethic. It is right to require of a man that he shall seek for the truth; but not that he shall find it. A speculative error, engendered in that huge storehouse of ignorance, human misunderstanding, ought not to annihilate in our minds the fervent admiration which every just and right-minded man ought to feel, and knows he ought to feel, of a life of constant goodness and continual self-sacrifice. All the actions of a man's life, harmonious in excellence as the planets in their orbits, should weigh something more than feathers in the scale, even if he is so far unfortunate as to be unable to solve the mystery of mysteries. It is not what we believe, but what we become, that is important to a man; and religion is but an instrument to ennoble the moral nature of man."

That is equally the purpose and mission of Masonry: " To diffuse useful information, to further intellectual refinement, to hasten the coming of the great day when the dawn of general knowledge shall chase away the lazy lingering mists, even from the base of the great social pyramid, is its high calling, in which the most splendid and consummate virtue may well press onward, eager to bear a part." And it is to be hoped that the time will soon arrive, for which Masonry has so long laboured, when, " as men will no longer suffer themselves to be led blindfold in ignorance, so will they no more yield to the vile principle of judging and treating their fellow creatures, not according to the intrinsic merit of their actions, but according to the accidental and involuntary coincidence of their opinion."

One of the earliest lessons taught the Masonic Initiate is, that every Masonic Temple, itself a symbol of the Universe, and of the soul of every upright and worthy man, is supported by three great columns, WISDOM, STRENGTH and BEAUTY or HARMONY. The inmost meanings of these three columns, I am not at liberty to make known here. They involve the highest truths of Philosophy and the profoundest Mysteries of Nature. When the Mason is advanced, however, to a certain point, he learns that these three pillars of the old Temple are replaced with three others, the names of which are familiar to you all - FAITH, HOPE and CHARITY— virtues which every Mason and every man and woman ought to possess: FAITH, - in God; that He is good and wise and merciful, a Father and not a Tyrant; whom we are as children to love, and not as slaves to fear; - in Human Nature; confidence in our kind, in the honesty of men's purposes and intentions; in man's capability for improvement and advancement; the same Faith in others that we would have them put in us, - and Faith in ourselves; - in our power to do some good, and exert some influence upon our fellows: Faith, that if we are but earnest, honest and sincere we can help destroy ignorance, error and wrong, and become immortal in our good influences living after we are dead; that noble and modest confidence in ourselves, which is the secret of all success, and the parent of all great and noble actions . . . HOPE, in the ultimate annihilation of Evil in the Universe in the final triumph of Masonry, that shall make of all men one family and household, in the cessation of war and bloodshed, and the advent of Peace and Liberty; in the final enfranchisement of the human soul and intellect in every country on the globe; and in a Hereafter, where man, immortal, shall be happy.... And CHARITY, taught us by Faith and Hope, for those who differ with us in opinion, for them and for their faith, and even for their errors; that Charity which relieves the necessities and distresses of men, and with open hand gives the suffering and destitute solace and comfort; and which forgives and utters merciful judgment upon the faults and short comings of others; believes them better than they seem, and teaches us to judge and do unto others as we should wish them, and think it right for them to judge and do unto us. To be TRUSTFUL, to be HOPEFUL, to be INDULGENT: - these, when all around us are selfishness, despondency, ill-opinion of

22

Human Nature, and Harsh and bitter judgment, are the true supports of every Masonic Temple, and the bases of every manly and heroic nature. And they are also the old pillars of the Temple under different names: for he only is Wise who judges others Charitably and deals with their errors Mercifully; he only is Strong, who is Hopeful; and there is no Beauty of proportion or harmony, like a firm Faith in God, our fellows and ourselves.

Our lectures say to us: The true Mason labours for the benefit of those that are to come after him, and for the advancement and improvement of his race. That is a poor ambition which contents itself within the limits if a single life. All men who deserve to live at all, desire to survive their own funerals, and to live afterwards in the good that they have done mankind, rather than in the writing which lasts even the longest upon the sands of human memories. Most men desire to leave some work behind them, that may outlive their day and brief generation. That is an instinctive impulse, given by God, and often found in the rudest human heart; the surest proof of the soul's immortality, and of the radical difference between man and the wisest brutes. To plant the trees that after we are dead shall shelter our children is as natural as to love the shade of those our fathers planted.

In his influences that survive him, man becomes immortal, before the general resurrection. The Thoughts of the Past are the Laws of the Present and Future. That which we say and do if its effects last not beyond our lives, is of slight importance. That which shall live when we are dead, as part of the great body of law enacted by the Dead is the only act worth doing, the only thought worth uttering. The desire to do something that shall benefit the world, when neither praise nor obloquy will reach us where we sleep soundly in the grave is the noblest ambition entertained by man To sow, that others may reap; to work and plant for those that are to occupy the earth when we are dead; to project our good influences far into the Future, and to live beyond our time; to rule as the Kings of Thought over men who are yet unborn; to bless with the glorious gifts of Truth and Light, and Liberty, those who may never know the name of the giver, nor care in what grave his unregarded ashes repose, is the true office of a Mason, and the proudest destiny of a man.

We read in Masonic Monitors, of Speculative Masonry, as distinguished from Operative Masonry. I confess I shall be glad to see it disused. It always seems to me to involve the idea of talking much, and doing nothing. Masonry is not speculative, but operative. It is work. Good Masonry is to do the work of life. Its natural work is practical life. Its precepts are meant for practical use. It was not meant for the lazy and luxurious, the indifferent or selfish. To long for the regeneration of the human race, and entertain a philanthropy that embraces the whole world, is very pleasant and very easy. The difficulty is, that when Masonry is no more than that, the field to be cultivated is so extensive, that no other crop is raised in any corner of it than weeds. It is a laudable ambition to wish to be the benefactor of the world, or at least of a nation; but most men can expect to be so, only through the influences they can exert within their own limited circle; and it would be too much, to expect your grand philanthropist, with universal Humanity for his client, to occupy himself with the pitiful interests of his own neighbourhood, and with the eradication of the evils that grow like poisonous rank weeds around his own door.

"The true Mason, on the contrary, occupies himself with what is near at hand. Right there he finds enough to do. His Masonry is to live a true, honourable, upright, affectionate life, from the motive of a good man. He finds evils enough, near him and around him, to be corrected; evils in trade, evils in social life, neighbourhood abuses; wrongs swarming everywhere, to be righted; follies cackling everywhere to be annihilated." "Masonry," it has been well said, " cannot, in our age, forsake the broad way of life. She must walk in the open street, appear in the crowded square, and teach men by her deeds, her life, more eloquent than any lips."

The Order says, in its charge to those who are to preside over its Lodges: "You are not to allow any assembly of the body over which you may preside, to close, without recalling to the minds of the brethren the duties of a Mason. That is an imperative duty. Forget not, that more than three thousand years ago, ZORO-ASTER said: Be good - be kind - be humane and charitable; love your fellows; console the afflicted; pardon those who have done you wrong ! Nor that more than two thousand three hundred years ago, CONFUCIUS repeated, also quoting the words of those who had lived before himself: " Love thy neighbour as thyself; Do not to others what thou wouldst not wish should be done to thyself; Forgive injuries; Forgive your enemy, be reconciled to him, give him assistance, invoke God in his behalf!"

"Let not the morality of your Lodge be inferior to that of the Persian or the Chinese Philosopher.

"Urge upon your brethren the teaching and the unostentatious practice of the morality of the Lodge, without regard to times, places, religions or peoples.

"Urge them to love one another, to be devoted to one another, to be faithful to the country, the Government and the laws; for to serve the country is to pay a dear and sacred debt.

"To respect all forms of worship, to tolerate all political and religious opinions- not to blame, and still less to condemn the religion of others; not to seek to make converts- but to be content if they have the religion of SOCRATES: - a veneration for the Creator, the religion of good works, and grateful acknowledgment of God's blessings.

"To fraternize with all men; to assist all who are unfortunate; and cheerfully to postpone their own interests to those of the Order.

"To make it the constant rule of their lives, to think well, to speak well, and to act well.

"To place the Sage above the Soldier, the Noble or the Prince; and take the wise and good as their models.

"To see that their professions and practice, their teachings and conduct do always agree.

"To make this also their motto: Do that which thou oughtest to do, let the result be what it will."

While Masonry inculcates these duties towards individuals, it also requires its initiates to work, actively and earnestly, for the benefit of their country. It is the Patron of the oppressed, as it is the comforter and consoler of the wretched and unfortunate. " It seems to it a worthier honour to be the instrument of advancement and reform, than to enjoy all that rank and office and lofty titles can bestow. It is the advocate of the common people, in those things which concern the best interests of mankind." It hates insolent power and impudent usurpation. It pities the poor, the sorrowing, the disconsolate. It would fain raise and improve the ignorant, the sunken and the degraded.

It is the Preacher of LIBERTY, FRATERNITY and EQUALITY: of a decent and well regulated liberty, based on law, and guarded by an inviolable constitution, under which the rights of the individual and the minority are as secure as those of the majority; of Liberty, that is not License, nor Anarchy, nor Licentiousness, nor the Despotism of party; and by which men are free, but not too free: of Fraternity, in that sober sense which regards men as the children of a common Father, to be loved when good, pitied and not hated when bad, persuaded and not persecuted when in error: Of Equality, in the eye of the Law, in political rights and in the rights of conscience.

But it is not its mission to engage in plots and conspiracies against the Civil Government. It is not the fanatical propagandist of any creed or theory; nor does it proclaim itself the general enemy of Kings. It contracts no entangling alliances with any Sect of Theorists, dreamers or political philosophers. It sits apart from all, in its own calm dignity and simplicity; the same in a Republic as under a Monarch; the same in Turkey as at the Rock of Plymouth; the same now as when the foundations of the first Temple at Jerusalem were laid.

It recognizes the truth of the proposition that necessity, as well as abstract ideal right and justice, plays a part in the making of laws, the administration of government and the regulation of relations in Society; and rules, in all the affairs of men. It knows that Freedom follows fitness for freedom as the consequence follows the cause; and that no people will be really free, until they are fit to govern themselves. Therefore, it does not preach sedition nor encourage rebellion by a people or a race, when it can only end in disaster and defeat; or if successful, in bloodshed and barbarism, and at last a worse servitude than before.

But wherever a people is fitted to be free, and generously strives to become so, there go all its sympathies. It hates and detests the Tyrant and the lawless oppressor, and him who abuses a lawful power. It frowns upon cruelty, and a wanton disregard of the rights of Humanity; and it is the enemy of the despotism of mob and autocrat alike. It is the votary of Liberty and Justice. Life's length, it tells its initiates, is not measured by its hours and days; but by that which we have done therein for our country and our kind. A useless life is short, if it last a century; but that of Alexander was long as the life of oaks, though he died at thirty-five. If we but eat and drink and sleep, and let everything go on around us at it pleases; or if we live but to amass wealth, or gain offices, or wear titles, we might as well not have lived at all.

In all times, Humanity has had three chief Enemies; the Despotism of ROYAL POWER, claiming to rule by Divine Right; the insolence, cruelty and bloodthirstiness of THE SACERDOTAL POWER, armed with the rack, the stake, and the gibbet; and the haughty pretensions of RANK, CASTE and PRIVILEGE, fenced about with exclusiveness and indignant when Truth and Right have seemed about to interfere with and diminish their "vested rights," by elevating the people to the dignity of manhood.

These three have always been the implacable enemies of Human Liberty ù and for many centuries the People gained ground, only when Pontiffs brought Kings to their knees, or the Throne had made against the insolent domineering of God's vicars; when the king ostracized and decimated his haughty nobles; or the nobles made concessions to the citizens and people, to enlist them against the crown.

Masonry was made to be THE ORDER OF THE PEOPLE. It has ever exerted its influence on the side of civil and religious liberty; of emancipation of both the muscles and the mind of all that were fit to be free; of education and enlightenment; of the elevation of the oppressed masses of Humanity to that level of Equality on which they ought to stand. Opposition to Regal Tyranny made the government of Masonry democratic; Hatred of Sacerdotal usurpation and intolerance dedicated its Lodges to the

Sts. John, opened its doors to men of all creeds, and closed them against sectarian discussions; and its adoption of a founder and worker in metals, the son of a poor Phoenician widow, as the Hero of its legend, evidences its hostility to the unjust privileges of oligarchies and aristocracies, and to Orders that by means of monopolies that weigh heavily on the shoulders of the people, live in luxurious and arrogant idleness.

It desires to see despotism everywhere dethroned, and constitutional government established in its place; the Sacerdotal Power of all Churches become like that which the Apostles exercised in the first days of Christianity; the ways to rank and civil employment, to office and honours, open to all whose merits and capacity entitle them to aspire: and therefore this now is, as it always was, its motto:

"Devotion to the interests of the People; detestation of Tyranny; sacred regard for the rights of Free Thought, Free Speech, and Free Conscience; implacable hostility to Intolerance, Bigotry, Arrogance and Usurpation; respect and regard for labour, which makes human nature noble; and scorn and contempt for all monopolies that minister to insolent and pampered luxury."

Bro. COUNT DE FERNIG said, in the Central Grand Lodge of the Scottish Rite in France, in 1843: "Man, frail and feeble, should be upheld by Scottish Masonry. It should elevate him, without changing his proper nature, or allowing him to become corrupted. It repudiates the dogma that commands the death of the Senses, as it rejects the Philosophy that exalts sensualism. It closes alike the books of Zeno and those of Epicurus. It believes in the Grand Architect of the universe, in the immortality of the soul, in the necessity of moderating and governing the human passions, to make of them human virtues.

"This is the substance of our precepts. Upon these bases the Supreme Council desires to erect that luminous Temple to which the Wise of every country and of all religions may repair.

"But to effect that, we must be convinced that no efforts

28

are insignificant, and no aid is unimportant. We are all fractions of the great Social Unit. We all play a part, more or less brilliant, more or less active, but always certain and always real, in this world. An edifice is not composed of great ashlars alone. There are materials of secondary appearance, which assist in producing its symmetry, its solidity and even its beauty. With us, too, nothing is without its use. It is necessary that every Brother should be a Mason, not only in the Lodge, but in the world; that he should preach as well by his example as with his lips; that he should cultivate wisdom, practice Fraternity, in its fullest sense, respect justice, and cause it to be respected; and then, whether he be an humble workman among the masses, or one who sits in the councils of kings, he will worthily have accomplished his task.

"Thus acting, we shall show that Masonry contains those fruitful germs, that it is for the interest of every Prince and of every country to seek to develop.

"When the founders of our Order exiled politics from our Temples, they were far from meaning that we ought to exercise no influence upon society; but they desired that this influence should be pure, sincere and moral. They fixed the seat of our power beyond the storms of the outer world, at he domestic hearth. They commanded us to make the man and the family better; for they knew that the power that forms habits and morals, dictates laws.

"They did not conceal it from themselves, that many generations must pass away, before the object would be attained. They knew the weaknesses also of the human heart. They knew that the children of the Grand Architect would wish to create, like Him, with a word and gesture, without the aid of Time, which alone makes fruitful and ripens. Haughty and unavailing desire! Let us have aims more moderate ! Let us learn to be patient, to be not discouraged, not to repine, if we do not see the work crowned with success, before we close our eyes upon this world I What is a single moment in Eternity ? And because the leaf drops upon the root, does the tree therefore cease to grow ? Let us again and again turn the furrows ploughed by our fathers, and the field will not become a field of tares ! "

At the same feast, the Bro. PHILIPPE DUPIN said: " At

Rome, the child who, born to Patrician rank, was destined to the perilous honours of the conduct of public affairs, seeing in the Atrium only the statues of his ancestors, their foreheads cinctured with triumphal coronets, was, as it were, reared under their eyes; and urged by their inspiring presence, he naturally rose to their level; at least he endeavoured to do so. In the same thought that antique adage of our fathers had its origin: NOBLESSE OBLIGE.

"So, my Brethren, while we study history, and contemplate the glorious past of those who lived and fought under our banners, let us too be nobly proud; and say, MACONNERIE OBLIGE! Yes, MASONRY is OBLIGATION! for it has been the forerunner of civilization. In its proscribed Temples, all the truths have found, sometimes a cradle, and sometimes a refuge: and when the world was vexed with savage virtues and stupid superstitions it purified beliefs, it raised altars to Toleration To Pity, to Justice, to all those holy Images that now gave light to the world. MACONNERIE OBLIGE: for when Intolerance furiously preached the worship of gods made by the hands of men it was in corporations, in secret societies, in Masonic Societies, that by the title of ' Grand Architect of the Universe,' a God was proclaimed Creator, Preserver and Supreme Judge of the human race. It was there that men learned to defend the great Principles of Liberty of Conscience and Free Thought; that is to say, the doctrine of improvement and progress, in relation both to the intellect and the heart, to intelligence and virtue. For that doctrine our fathers fought. The struggle was fierce, sanguinary, glorious. You have your Heroes Sages, Martyrs. You possess the immense glory of having triumphed for the happiness of all.

"But now, when the hand of Intolerance is no longer armed with the steel, when your Temples have august protectors, and society walks in your paths, are you to conclude that Masonry has lived its time, accomplished its task, and may rest from its labours ? Are we now to seek in indolent repose the reward of our toils ? That would be to mistake at once the object of the Institution, the condition of society, and the demands of the generous mission to which we have devoted ourselves.

"When the despotism of blind superstition was tyrant over the world, Masonry, naked of material power, ruled and reigned in the domain of ideas; protested for the present, and sought to enlighten the future. Now in the elevated sphere it occupies, it should still reign and rule, to complete its work, perhaps by a different course. Thus men's beliefs are no longer rude and savage, and Masonry does not need to soften and combat them; but now, that creeds have become enfeebled and emasculated by the mere effect of civilization, is it not the noble duty of Masonry to endeavour to give them new life and vigour, and to develop what in them is true, consolatory, just, useful and venerable ? You have heretofore set limits to all excesses, and you ought to do so again: you should maintain order in institutions, among men, in ideas; and precisely because you have heretofore warred against excesses and errors that were to be deplored, it is now your mission to war against excesses and errors in the opposite direction.

"You profess, as the basis of your doctrine, the law of Equality, of Fraternity among men, of Liberty for all; but you ought also to teach all men the true meaning and representative value of those words, which may enlighten and instruct but may also lead astray and bewilder; for you, by your studies, and by the practical life of your Lodges have learned what they mean and what they command.

"To you, as to all men of progress, the word ' Equality ' means Equality as of right, for equal virtues and equal capacities; a share in the same advantages, for those who, by equal titles deserve them. To understand it in any other sense, is contrary to the principles of morality and justice, and to the teachings of Nature herself.

"Does it not belong to you, who have always been the defenders of liberty, to declare the austere duties which it imposes on all; and to demonstrate that it can have no solid basis, unless it be built upon virtue and respect of the rights of others ? Does not the voice of Masonry still need to incite to fraternal union all men and every people ? That is its mission. It embraces the two Hemispheres in the vast circle of fraternal beneficence. For your sphere of action is not narrowed and limited by the frontiers of this realm. Masonry is of all countries, as she is of all times."

As long ago as 1741, the Grand Master, the DUC D'ANTIN, said: "The whole world is only one Republic, of which every nation is a family, and every individual a child. The sublime art of Masonry, without interfering with the different duties which the diversity of States exacts, tends to create a new People, which, made up from many nations, cements them all, as it were, together by the cohesive power of Science, Morality and Virtue." Time has enabled us to improve but little upon this definition.

The answer to the inquiry, what Masonry is would be very incomplete, if nothing were said of its philosophy; and yet I have time to say but little.

Masonry is as little a religious sect as it is a political party. As it embraces all parties, so it embraces all sects, to form from among them all a vast fraternal association. The morals of antiquity, of the law of Moses, and of Christianity, are ours. We recognize every teacher of Morality, every Reformer, as a Brother. No one Mason has the right to measure for another, within the walls of a Masonic Temple, the degree of veneration which he shall feel for any Reformer, or the Founder of any Religion. We teach a belief in no particular creed, as we teach un-belief in none. In all religions there is a basis of Truth, in all there are fragments at least of pure Morality. All that teach the cardinal tenets of Masonry, we respect; all teachers and reformers of mankind, we admire and revere.

We do not undervalue the importance of any Truth. We utter no word that can be deemed irreverent by anyone of any faith. We do not tell the Moslem that it is only important for him to believe that there is but one God, and wholly unessential whether Mahomet was his prophet. We do not tell the Hebrew that the Messiah whom he expects was born in Bethlehem nearly two thousand years ago, and substituted a better faith in the place of the law of Moses. And as little do we tell the sincere Christian that Jesus of Nazareth was but a man like us, or his history but the unreal revival of an older legend. To do either, is beyond our jurisdiction. Masonry of no one age, belongs to all time; of no religion, it finds its great truths in all.

It is not disbelief nor scepticism. It has its own creed, simple and sublime, to which every good man of every religion can

32

assent. It expounds all the old philosophies, and modestly and not oracularly utters its own.

To every Mason, there is a God - ONE, SUPREME, INFI- NITE in Goodness, in Wisdom, Foresight, Justice and Benevo- lence; CREATOR, DISPOSER and PRESERVER of all things. How, or by what Intermediates, Powers or Emanations He creates and acts, and in what way He unfolds and manifests Himself, Ma- sonry leaves to Creeds and Religions to inquire.

To every Mason, the soul of man is immortal. Whether it emanated from, and will return to God and what is to be its contin- ued mode of existence hereafter, each judges for himself. Masonry was not made to settle that.

To every Mason, WISDOM or INTELLIGENCE FORCE or STRENGTH, and HARMONY, or FITNESS PROPORTION and BEAUTY, are the Trinity of the Attributes of God. With the subtle- ties of Philosophy and Scholasticism concerning them, Masonry does not meddle, nor decide as to the reality of the supposed Exis- tences that are their Personifications nor whether the Christian's Trinity be such a Personification, or a Reality of the gravest import and significance.

To every Mason, the Infinite Justice and Benevolence of God give ample assurance that Evil will ultimately be dethroned, and the Good, the True and the Beautiful reign triumphant and eternal. It teaches that Evil and Pain and Sorrow exist as parts of a wise and beneficent plan, all the parts of which work together under God's eye, to a result which will be perfection. Whether the existence of Evil is rightly explained in this creed or in that; by Typhon, the Great Serpent, by Ahriman and his army of wicked spirits; by the Giants and Titans warring against Heaven; by the two co-existent, co- eternal principles of Good and Evil; by Satan's temptation and the fall of man; it is beyond the domain of Masonry to decide, and it does not even inquire. Nor is it within its province to determine how the ultimate triumph of Light and Truth and Good, over Darkness and Error and Evil is to be achieved.

Thus it disbelieves no truth, and teaches unbelief in no

creed except so far as such creed may lower its own lofty estimate of the Deity, degrade him to the level of the passions of Humanity, deny the high destiny of man, impugn God's goodness and infinite benevolence, strike at the great columns of Masonry, CHARITY, HOPE and FAITH, or inculcate immorality, and disregard of the active duties of life.

It is not a religion, but a WORSHIP; and one in which all civilized men can unite; for it does not undertake to explain, or dogmatically to settle those great mysteries, that are above the feeble comprehension of our human intellect. It trusts in God, and HOPES: it BELIEVES, like a child, and is humble: It draws no sword to compel others to adopt its belief or be happy with its hopes: And it WAITS with patience to understand the mysteries of nature and nature's God hereafter.

The first great Truth in Masonry is: No man hath seen God at any time. He is ONE, ETERNAL, All-powerful, All-wise, Infinitely Just, Merciful, Benevolent and Compassionate; Creator and Preserver of all things, the Source of Light and Life, co-extensive with Time and Space, Eternal as one and Infinite as the other; Who thought, and with the thought created the Universe, and all living things, and the Souls of Men: THAT WHICH IS: the PERMANENT: while everything besides Him is a perpetual Genesis: That His Justice, Wisdom and Mercy are alike infinite, alike perfect, and yet do not in the least jar or conflict one with the other:

While the first oaks still put forth their leaves, man lost the perfect knowledge of the One True God, the ancient absolute EXISTENCE, the Infinite MIND and Supreme INTELLIGENCE; and floated helplessly out upon the shoreless ocean of conjecture. Then the Intellect vexed and tortured itself with seeking to learn whether the material universe was a mere chance combination of atoms, or the work of Infinite uncreated wisdom: . . . whether everything Material and Spiritual was created by the Deity out of nothing; or whether matter and He were co-existent, and creation only the moulding into shape of chaos: . . . whether the universe was God, or God was the soul of the Universe, pervading every part of it; or an independent existence, separate and apart from the Universe; a personal Existence; . . . whether with ever-present and ever-recurring immediate personal action He produces the contin-

34

ual succession of phenomena and effects; or whether those effects are but the results of an unchangeable law enacted by Him in the remote ages of Eternity. All their Philosophies, struggle as they might to avoid the perilous abyss, ended in one of the two conclusions: either that there is no God, or that all that exists is God - in theoretical Atheism or Pantheism; and so they wandered ever deeper into the darkness and were lost, and there was for them no longer any real God, but only a great dumb Universe.

Atheism, it is true, never was more than a theory. " It has been said," a great Thinker writes, " Death is the end: this is a world without a God ù There is no Providence: Nature is a fortuitous concourse of atoms; thought is a fortuitous function of matter a fortuitous result of a fortuitous result, a chance shot from the great wind gun of the Universe, accidentally loaded, pointed at random, and shot off by chance. Things happen; they are not arranged. There is luck, and there is ill-luck; but there is no Providence. There is only a Universe all disorder: no Infinite, no Reason, no Conscience, no Heart no Soul of things; nothing to reverence, to esteem, to love, to worship, to trust in; but only an ugly FORCE, alien and foreign to us, that strikes down those we love, and makes us mere worms on the hot sand of the world. Out of the sky smiles no kind Providence, in all its thousand starry eyes; and in storms, a malignant VIOLENCE, with its lightning sword, stabs into the darkness, seeking for men to murder."

Man never could be content with that - to believe that there was no Mind that thought for man, no Conscience to enact eternal laws, no Heart to love those whom nothing of earth loves or cares for, no Will of the Universe to marshal the nations in the way of Justice, wisdom and love. History is not the fortuitous concourse of events, or nature that of atoms. He cannot believe that there is no plan nor purpose in nature, to guide our going out or coming in; that there is a mighty going, but it goes nowhere; that all beauty, wisdom, affection, justice and morality in the world, is an accident, and may end to-morrow.

All that is well and truly said. Masonry admits its truth, and not only requires of the aspirant within its Temples to profess a belief in the existence of a God; but before he is made a Mason, to unite in prayer to Him, and declare that in Him he puts his trust.

35

With that it is for the time content; but afterwards it endeavours to communicate to him adequate and rational ideas of the Grand Architect of the Universe; that honour the Deity and are not idolatry.

Most truly it was said: " It is not profanity to deny the Deity of the ignorant vulgar, but to assign to Him the attributes imagined by them is profanity." Most truly it has been said: " Verily, verily, travellers have seen many monstrous idols in many countries; but no human eyes have ever beheld more daring, gross and shocking images of the Divine nature, than we creatures of the dust make in our own likenesses, of our own bad passions, impiously reversing the order of creation, and breathing our own spirit into a mental image and idol of the Creator.

So it has been truly said by another, that " every religion and every conception of God is idolatrous, in so far as it is imperfect; and as it substitutes a feeble and temporary idea in the shrine of that Undiscoverable Being, who can be known only in part, and who can therefore be honoured, even by the most enlightened among his worshippers, only in proportion to their limited powers of understanding and imagining to themselves His perfections .
"

No symbol of Deity can be appropriate or durable, except in a relative or moral sense. We cannot exalt words that have only a sensuous meaning, above sense. To call Him a POWER, or a FORCE, or an INTELLIGENCE, is merely to deceive ourselves into the belief that we use words that have a meaning to us; while really they have no more than the ancient visible symbols had. To call him SOVEREIGN, FATHER, GRAND ARCHITECT OF HEAVEN AND EARTH; EXTENSION; TIME; BEGINNING, MIDDLE AND END; WHOSE FACE IS TURNED ON ALL SIDES; THE SOURCE OF LIFE AND DEATH; is but to hold out to other men certain mental symbols, by which we in vain endeavour to communicate to them the same vague ideas which men in all ages have impotently struggled to express, and it may be doubted whether we have succeeded, either in communicating, or in forming in our own minds, any more distinct and definite, and true and adequate ideas of the Deity, in any other than His moral aspect, with all our metaphysical conceits and logical subtleties, than the rude ancients did, who endeavoured to symbolize, and so to express His attributes, by the Fire, the

Light, the Sun and Stars, the Lotus and the Scarabaus; all of them types, of what, except by types, more or less sufficient, could not and cannot be expressed at all.

The Heathen Gods were unrealities, and mere ideal personifications, either of the Heavenly Bodies, the Powers of Nature, or the Principles of light and Darkness, Good and Evil. The ancients worshipped the Powers of Nature in the constellation, and the constellations in the animals imaged there. But always there were a few who believed that there was but one only True God, who has no bodily shape, and hath never been seen by any man; who is not the Light nor the Fire; but pure absolute Intellect and Existence; a Personality, existing before the Universe, which He created with a Thought; that the Past, the Present and the illimitable Future, the infinite series of events and successions of Time in both directions are all present to Him at one and the same moment. There is to HIM no FUTURE; and no PAST. He is present everywhere, and there is to HIM neither THERE nor ELSEWHERE; but everything, to Him, is HERE and Now; that He is necessarily unchangeable, immutable, infinitely just, wise and powerful, yet infinitely merciful, loving and benevolent; and can neither be angry nor repent.

And so Masonry says to its Initiates this: " God is One; Unapproachable, Single, Eternal and Unchanging; and not that Supposed God of Nature, whose manifold power was imagined to be immediately revealed to the Senses in the incessant round of movement, life and death.

"The MANIFOLD is an infinite illustration of the One. The Forces of Nature are the laws enacted by the absolute Uncreated Existence. In the absence of Creation by Him, no attribute could have been appended to His name. By the Emanations of His Omnipotence we become conscious of His abstract Being, and the ELOHIM, by which He created all that is, are His creative powers, and a part of those Emanations.

"All the Gods of the Heathen are false idols; because being but men's attributes and passions enlarged and personified, they are wholly unreal and have no existence. There is but one God, infinite and incomprehensible, to whom no human attribute can be prop-

37

erly assigned, even when imagined to be infinite.

"The POWERS of God are not Persons nor Beings distinct from Him, but His THOUGHTS, immaterial as our Thoughts, and existing in Him, as Thoughts exist in our own Souls.

"God is the Soul of the Universe, distinct from and superior to the Universe of things, as the Soul of man is distinct from and superior to his frail body.

"There is no rival God ever at war with THE INEFFABLE; nor any independent and self-existent Evil Principle in rebellion against Him. The Universe is a great whole, in which everything tends to a good result, through an infinite series of things; like a great harmony in which discords and concords mingle, and which, without either, would be imperfect."

Man, his intellect too limited to comprehend these mysteries, must believe; and simple faith is wiser than all the vain speculations of Philosophy.

Let him steer far away from all those vain Philosophies, that endeavour to account for all that is, without admitting that there is a God, separate and apart from the Universe, which is His work; that erect Universal Nature into a God, and worship it alone; that annihilate spirit, and believe no testimony except that of the bodily senses; that by logical formulas and dexterous collocation of words make the actual, living, guiding and protecting God fade into the dim mistiness of a mere abstraction and unreality, itself a mere logical formula.

In all ages, the golden threads of Truth have gleamed in the woof of Error. Fortunate the Mason, who, by the Light of Wisdom, the True Masonic LIGHT, first Emanation from the Deity, can discern the golden threads, God's hieroglyphics, written when Time began; and read them aright, as they were read by our Ancient Brethren in the early ages!

Thus in all ages the WORD OF GOD, His THOUGHT, the Great Creative Power, not spoken through material organs nor in a voice audible to mortal ears, has sounded in the souls of men, and taught them the great Truths of Reason, Philosophy and Religion.

Fortunate the Mason, to whom that WORD, the Deity Manifest, is audible, intelligible, significant; God's THOUGHT, that made the Stars, and all that is, and the Great Laws of Harmony and Motion.

In all ages, rosy gleams of light, tinging the dark clouds of Error, have taught mankind that Truth and Light, perfect and glorious, linger below the Horizon of Mortal Vision, in time to rise, like the Sun, and all God's Universe with light and glory, at the Dawn of His appointed day. Fortunate the Mason, who with firm faith and hope accepts these struggling rays that gild the clouds, as ample evidence that, in God's good time, His Dawn of day will come, and be eternal!

The existence of a God, who is the immaterial soul of the Universe, present in it everywhere, and yet wholly distinct from it, is a mystery beyond our comprehension; but no more so than the existence of the soul of man, the advent of light to the earth from the remotest stars, after journeying many thousand years, the presence of latent electricity and heat in the most solid bodies: - and the existence of a Soulless Universe, without a God and un-created by a God, would be a greater mystery, and more incom-prehensible still.

The idea that God never began to exist, but always was, is one beyond our comprehension, and which the soul struggles in vain to grasp; but not more so than the idea of space infinite in ex-tent, and time infinite in duration: - and it would be a far greater mystery, if, after an eternity, during which there had been no God, during which there had been everywhere in infinite space blank nothingness; never during a whole eternity of Time an echo of a Thought; God, without a cause, had begun to be.

That the Thought and Will of God, uttered in the word, are an infinite omnipotent Power of Creation and Production, of Pres-ervation and Destruction, that brought into existence out of Noth-ingness, the whole infinite Universe of Worlds, is a mystery, the greatest of all mysteries, we are in the habit of thinking; but it is as comprehensible as the existence of a Soul, of a Thought that can separate itself from and go out of the Soul, that can live after the utterer is dead- that is an actual Power, and moulds the fates, and influences the destinies, of Humanity: - and it would be a greater

39

mystery still, if the material Universe, not instinct with a Soul, nor having a Creator, and without a Producing Cause, had existed always, or had sprung into existence itself.

The action of the will of one man on the conduct of another; the unknown, invisible, immaterial power that draws the magnet round with irresistible energy to the North the development of the acorn into the oak, the phenomena of dreams are equally mysteries and equally incomprehensible to us. God is a mystery, only as everything that surrounds us is; and as we are mysteries to ourselves.

GOD LIVES, AND IS IMMORTAL. His Thought, that created, preserves. It conducts and controls the Universe, all spheres, all words, all actions of mankind, and of every animate and inanimate creature. It speaks in the soul of every man that lives. The Stars, the Earth, the Trees, the Winds, the universal voice of Nature, Tempest and Avalanche, the Sea's roar and the grave voice of the Waterfall, the hoarse thunder, and the soft whisper of the brook, the ice mountains sailing in Northern Seas, the song of birds, the voices of Love, the speech of Men, all are the alphabet in which it communicates itself to men, and informs them on the will and law of God, " who made and blesses all."

Before the world grew old, the primitive Truth and Knowledge faded out of men's minds. Then man asked himself: "What am I? and how and whence am I? and whither do I go?" And the soul, looking inward upon itself, endeavoured to learn whether that " I," that was conscious of its own individuality and identity, were mere matter, its thought, reason, passions and affections mere results of material combination- or whether it were an Immaterial existence, enveloped in, and environed by the impediments of, matter; whether it were an individual essence, complete and perfect by itself, with a separate and inherently immortal life; or an infinitesimal portion of a great FIRST PRINCIPLE or UNIVERSAL SOUL, that interpenetrates the Universe, extends through the infinitudes of space, and undulates like light and heat; and so they wandered further and further on amid the mazes of Error, and imagined vain philosophies wallowing in the sloughs of materialism and sensualism, or vainly beating their wings in the vacuum of abstractions and idealities.

40

But Masonry teaches us that the soul of man is immortal; not the mere result of organization, nor an aggregate of modes of action of matter; not a mere succession of phenomena and perceptions; but an EXISTENCE, one and identical, a Living Spirit, a spark from the Great Central Light, that hath entered into and dwells in the body, to be separated from it at death, and return to God who gave it; that does not disperse or vanish at death, like breath or a smoke, nor can be annihilated; but still exists and possess activity and intelligence, even as it existed in God before it was enveloped in the body. It is immortal, not of necessity, but, unless, as it and all things emanated from God, it pleases Him to absorb it again unto Himself.

We do not understand this; but we believe. We struggle to express the Truth, by words that are inadequate. Far in the darkened Past we hear our Ancient Brethren, with stammering utterance, striving to express the same idea of immortality, saying:

"The seed dies, and out of its death springs the young shoot of the new wheat, to produce an hundredfold.

"The worm dies in its narrow prison house, woven by itself; and out of its death springs the brilliant moth, emblem of immortality.

"The long lived serpent dies, and self-renews its own existence; and out of the death of night's sleep, the minor mystery, comes the renewed life of the morning.

"Now, as ever, out of death springs Life; out of Darkness ever awakes the Light; and to Evil in eternal circle Good succeeds."

It is the great problem of Human Existence, whether the Power and Principle of Good is ultimately to dethrone and destroy the Power and Principle of Evil; whether pain and calamity and sin and sorrow are hereafter to disappear from the Universe, and all thenceforward be Light and Joy and Content and Happiness; whether there is another life, in which the malign influences of the Demon of Evil will be unfelt, and where reparation will be made for the sufferings of Virtue, and the calamities of the good, in this life: for it is the Great Problem whether we are better than the brutes that perish; and whether there is a Great, Good, Beneficent FATHER in Heaven, who will in His own good time connect together all the thousand links of circumstance, and make them lead to one good and excellent result.

The laws which control and regulate the Universe, are those of MOVEMENT and HARMONY. We see only the isolated incidents of things, and cannot, with our feeble and limited capacity and vision discern their connection, nor the mighty chords that make the apparent discord perfect harmony. Evil is merely apparent; and all is in reality good and perfect. For pain and sorrow, persecution and calamity, affliction and destitution, sickness and death, are but the means by which alone the noblest virtues can be developed. Without them, and without error and sin, and injury and outrage, as there can be no effect without an adequate cause, there could be neither patience nor prudence, nor temperance, nor courage to meet danger; nor truth, when to speak it is hazardous; nor love that lives despite ingratitude; nor charity, nor forbearance and forgiveness, nor toleration, nor charitable judgment of men's motives and actions; nor patriotism, nor heroism, nor self denial, nor generosity. Human virtues and excellencies would have no existence, their very names be unknown, their natures be entirely incomprehensible to us. Life would be one low, flat, dead level, above which none of the lofty elements of human nature would emerge, and man would lie lapped in contented indolence and apathetic idleness, a mere worthless negative, instead of the brave, strong soldier against the grim legions of Evil and of rude Difficulty.

The Laws of Nature are the development of LOVE the Universal Law, the Divine motive for Creation. Hence flow attraction and affinities, and the swift flash of the Electric Current; the tides, the clouds, the movements of the world, the influence of will and the mysterious power of magnetism. Nature is one great HARMONY; and of that Harmony, every human soul is a tone. From God it flows in never ceasing circles, as Light and Splendour from his Sun. To Him the notes of that harmony return, and mingle with the mighty diapason of the spheres, and are immortal.

Man is not governed by a resistless blind FATE or inexorable dumb DESTINY; but is FREE to choose between Evil and the Good. We are conscious of our freedom to act, as we are conscious of our existence and continuing identity. " We have the same evidence of one as of the other; if we can put one in doubt, we have no certainty of either, and everything is unreal; and we can deny our free will and free agency, only upon the ground that they are in the nature of things impossible; which would be to deny the Omnipotence of God."

THE MYSTERIES OF THE GREAT UNIVERSE OF GOD I How can we with our limited mental vision, expect to grasp and comprehend them? Infinite SPACE, stretching out from us every way, without limit; infinite TIME, without beginning or end; and we, HERE and Now, in the centre of each: an infinity of Suns, the nearest of which only diminish in size, viewed with the most powerful telescope; each with its retinue of worlds; some that we seem; to see, whose light that now reaches our eyes has been upon its journey for fifty centuries our world spinning upon its axis, and rushing ever in its circuit round the sun; and it, with the sun and all our special system revolving round some great central point; and that and suns, stars and worlds evermore flashing onward with inconceivable rapidity through illimitable space- - and then, in every drop of water that we drink, incredible multitudes of living creatures, invisible to the naked eye, of a minuteness beyond belief, yet organized, living, feeding, devouring each the other; no doubt with consciousness of identity, and memory and instinct.

Such are the mysteries of the great Universe of God; and yet we would fain know by what process He created it; would understand His Powers, His Attributes, His Emanations, His mode of existence and Action- the plan according to which all events proceed - that plan profound as God himself; would know the laws by which He controls the Universe; would fain see and talk to Him face to face; and are unwilling to believe what we do not understand.

He commands us to love one another, to become like little children. He tells us that to love Him and to love our neighbour are the great commandments, obeying which we shall live; and we dis-

43

pute and wrangle, and hate and persecute each other because we cannot all be of one opinion as to His Essence, or agree upon a complete inventory of His attributes, or believe that this doctrine or that is heresy or truth; drenching the world with blood, depopulating realms, and turning fertile lands into deserts, for the glory of God and to vindicate the truth; until, for religious wars, persecutions and murders, the Earth for many a century has rolled round the Sun, a charnel house, steaming and reeking with human gore, the blood of brother slain by brother for opinion's sake, that has soaked into and polluted all her veins, and made her a horror to her Sisters of the Universe.

And if all men had always obeyed with all their heart, the mild and gentle teachings of Masonry, that world would always have been a paradise; while Intolerance and Persecution make of it a hell. For this is the Masonic creed: BELIEVE, in God's infinite benevolence, wisdom and justice; Hope, for the final triumph of good over evil, and for Perfect Harmony as the final result of all the concords and discords of the Universe; and be CHARITABLE, as God is, towards the unfaith, the errors, the follies and the faults of men; for all are one great Brotherhood.

Made in the USA
San Bernardino, CA
31 May 2018